MASTER YOUR FOCUS

A PRACTICAL GUIDE TO STOP CHASING THE NEXT THING AND FOCUS ON WHAT MATTERS UNTIL IT'S DONE (PERSONAL WORKBOOK)

THIBAUT MEURISSE

How to use this workbook

This workbook is to be used together with the book "Master Your Focus: A Practical Guide to Stop Chasing the Next Thing and Focus on What Matters Until It's Done (Personal Workbook)."

If you haven't grabbed "Master Your Focus", you can get it at the URL below:

http://mybook.to/master_focus

I encourage you to complete all the exercises in this workbook. The more effort you put into it, the better results you'll get.

Let's get started, shall we?

PART I
WHAT FOCUS IS AND WHY IT MATTERS

The different type of focuses

Rate your short-term, transitional and long-term focus on a scale of 1 to 10

#1 Short-term focus (concentration)

0 _____ 10

#2 Transitional focus (planning/routine)

0 _____ 10

#3 Long-term focus (vision)

0 _____ 10

Focus and productivity

How often do you find yourself in each of the productivity level below (1 being never, 10 very often)

1. Procrastinating

0 _____ 10

2. Working on the wrong things

0 _____ 10

3. Working on things that don't improve your life

0 _____ 10

4. Working on the right things

0 _____ 10

5. Working on the right things the right way

0 _____ 10

What one simple action could you take today to spend more time working on the right things?

PART II
KNOWING WHAT YOU WANT

15 questions to develop clarity

Answer the questions below as honestly as possible.

1. Electing desire

1) What do you really, really want?

2) If you were to wake up tomorrow, completely alone without any family member, friend or colleague to influence your decisions, what would you do differently?

_____
_____
_____
_____
_____
_____

3) If you were to be honest with yourself, what would you start doing now? What would you stop doing?

_____
_____
_____
_____
_____
_____

4) If you were guaranteed to succeed in everything you do, where would you want to be in three years from now?

_____

_____

_____

_____

_____

_____

5) If you could spend your day exactly the way you wanted to, what would you be doing from morning to night? What would your ideal day consist of?

_____

_____

_____

_____

_____

_____

6) If you could focus only on doing one thing for the rest of your life, what would it be?

_____

_____

_____

_____

_____

_____

7) If you understood and truly believed you could achieve absolutely anything you want by sticking to it for long enough, what would you pursue in the next three to five years?

_____

_____

_____

_____

_____

_____

2. Finding your strengths and unique abilities

8) When are you the happiest at work and what are you doing?

_____

_____

_____

_____

_____

_____

9) What do you find so easy to do you genuinely wonder why others struggle to do the same thing?

_____

_____

_____

_____

_____

_____

10) What do people around you say you're great at?

Feel free to email your family, friends or colleagues using the template below.

Hi____,

I hope you're doing well.

I'm trying to identify my strengths so I can leverage them to design a more fulfilling career and life. I really need outside perspectives on what you consider I am really good at.

I'd appreciate if you could provide me with honest feedback and give me a list of the strengths you think I have.

Please don't be afraid to tell me anything that comes to mind.

Thanks so much for your support.

Warm regards,

To learn how to find your strengths I encourage you to check out my free book "Find What You Love: 5 Tips to Find Your Passion Quickly and Easily" at:

http://whatispersonaldevelopment.org/find-what-you-love

3. Uncovering your passion

11) What did you enjoy doing when you were a kid?

_____

_____

_____

_____

_____

_____

12) Who do you envy and why?

_____

_____

_____

_____

_____

_____

13) If you had all the time and money in the world, what would you do?

_____

_____

_____

_____

_____

_____

14) If you had complete confidence and were already your absolute best self, what would you be doing with your life?

_____

_____

_____

_____

_____

_____

15) How do you want to express yourself to the world? Do you want to entertain, educate, inspire, heal, teach, or create? What emotions do you want people to feel when in your presence?

_____

_____

_____

_____

_____

_____

4. Clarifying your values

Write down your list of top ten values using the list below: https://jamesclear.com/core-values

Your values should be specific and non-negotiable.

1.

2.

3.

4.

5.

6.

7.

8.

9.

10.

Creating a compelling vision

Write down where you want to be in ten years in all areas of your life. Your vision doesn't have to be perfect. Just make sure you spend some time thinking about it and answering the questions below in writing.

What does your ideal career look like?

_____
_____
_____
_____
_____
_____

What kind of relationship do you want to be in?

_____
_____
_____
_____
_____
_____

How do you want your health to be like?

___

What does your social life look like?

___

What emotional states do you want to experience every day?

___

Now, what do you need to focus on every day/week/year to make your vision a reality?

_____

_____

_____

_____

_____

Strengthening your why

Come up with at least 20 reasons why your vision must become a reality. Make sure they are aligned with your values and/or four motivators (love, desire, ego and pain).

1.

2.

3.

4.

5.

6.

7.

8.

9.

10.

11.

12.

13.

14.

15.

16.

17.

18.

19.

20.

PART III
PLANNING EFFECTIVELY

Breaking down your vision

Break down your vision into yearly, 90-day, weekly and daily goals. Make sure your goals are SMART.

As a reminder, SMART stands for:

- **Specific**: What exactly do you want? What are you trying to achieve?
- **Measurable**: Can you assess the progress towards your goal easily? How will you know whether you've achieved it?
- **Achievable**: Is it achievable? Is the timeframe realistic? Can you put in the effort required despite other responsibilities?
- **Relevant**: Is it in line with your values? Is it exciting you?
- **Time-bound**: Do you have a clear deadline for your goals?

Yearly goals

What milestones do you need to reach this year to move closer to your vision?

Process goals:

_____

_____

_____

Result goals :

90-day goals

To create a 90-day goal:

- Define the few key tasks you must accomplish by the end of the 90 day
- Write them down. You always want to work from a written plan.
- Review your 90-day goals daily.
- Put in place an accountability system.

So, what milestones do you need to reach in the next 90 days to achieve your yearly goals?

Process goals:

_____

_____

_____

_____

Result goals:

_____

_____

_____

_____

Weekly goals

What milestones do you need to reach this week to achieve your 90 days goal?

Process goals:

_____

_____

_____

_____

Result goals:

_____

_____

_____

_____

Daily goals

What can you do today to achieve your weekly goals?

Process goals:

_____

_____

_____

_____

Result goals:

_____

_____

_____

_____

PART IV
DEVELOPING A RUTHLESS FOCUS

1. Prioritizing

Answer the following questions:

1) If the time you had available was reduced by 95% what task(s) would you still perform?

_____

_____

_____

_____

2) If it were up to you, what activities or goals would you dump right away?

_____

_____

_____

_____

3) If you had to drop any activities or goals that aren't a resounding yes for you, which ones would you drop?

_____

_____

_____

_____

4) What are you spending time doing merely because you're fooling yourself?

_____

_____

_____

_____

5) What activities or projects can you put on hold for now?

_____

_____

_____

_____

6) If you could focus only on one thing in the coming twelve months and had to let go of everything else, albeit temporarily, which one would make the biggest impact in your life?

_____

7) What activities are generating uncertain or unconvincing results while draining much of your energy?

_____

_____

_____

_____

8) Knowing what you know now, if you were to start all over again today, which current activities, projects or goals would you choose to drop?

_____

_____

_____

_____

_____

2. Approaching a task the correct way

Refer to this 7 steps before starting a new task.

Step 1. Prioritizing my task

- If I could do only one thing today, what task would have the most impact?
- Is this task moving me closer to my main goal?
- Do I really need to do it right now?

Step 2. Assessing the validity of my task

- Do I *really* need to do this task?
- Is right now the best timing?
- Do I work on it because I need to or because it makes me feel good?

Step 3. Clarifying what needs to be done

- What exactly do I need to do here?
- What does the finished product look like?

Step 4. Determining whether I should be the one doing it

- Is this task really worth my time?
- Is there anyone who could do it better than me? If so, can I ask for help?
- What would happen if I simply remove/postpone this task?
- Do I enjoy working on this task?

Step 5. Finding out the most effective way to tackle that task

- What tool(s) can I use, people can I ask or method can I rely on to complete that task as fast as possible?
- What skill could I learn or improve to complete this task faster in the future?

Step 6. Batching the task with other similar tasks

- Can I batch that task with other similar tasks?

Step 7. Automatizing/systematizing your task

- Can I create templates I can reuse every time I work on that task or similar ones?
- Can I create checklists?

3. Making the right domino falls

What is ONE key decision that if you are to take today would make it easier for you to achieve most of your goals?

_____

What is ONE daily habit that if you are to adopt today would make it easier for you to achieve most of your goals?

_____

30-day challenge

Commit to sticking to your new habit for 30 days in a row.

4. The power of less

A. Having fewer goals

Look at the 90-day goals you previously created. Now, what goal(s) could you postpone or eliminate?

_____

_____

_____

What goal(s) do you want to focus more on?

_____

_____

_____

B. Removing things from your life

Write down below a list of all activities you engage in during your typical week.

-
-
-
-
-
-
-
-
-
-
-
-

What is ONE thing that, if I were to stop doing, would release the most pressure on my shoulders?

_____

What would it take for you to stop doing that thing?

_____
_____
_____
_____
_____
_____

Saying "no"

Practice saying no more often. Remember the following:

- Start small
- Stop over-justifying yourself
- Practice say no using role-play
- Try the "say no challenge" by saying no to everything for two weeks.

D. Having fewer distractions

Identify distracting activities

Write down all activities that have a strong potential for distraction

-

-

-

-

-

-

-

Undertake a digital detox

Undertake a 7-day digital detox by:

- Scheduling blocks of time for your distractions. To do so batch non-productive activities together. For instance, you can have two blocks of time per day during which you'll check your social media, emails etc.
- Avoid checking your digital devices first thing in the morning and focus on your key activities instead (see 30-day challenge)

5. Scheduling everything

Are you easily distracted? Write down how you react in the following situations:

When you receive a phone call:

_____
_____
_____
_____

When someone asks you for help/a question:

_____
_____
_____
_____

Now, answer the questions below:

If you perceived your time as the most valuable resources in the world, how would you act differently in your daily life?

_____
_____
_____
_____

What are three things you can do to reclaim control over your day?

1.

2.

3.

Schedule interrupted block of times.

Starting this week, schedule at least one interrupted block of time to work on your most important task. Write what you will work on, for how long and when:

What I will work on:

_____
_____
_____
_____

How long I will work on it:

_____
_____
_____
_____

When exactly (day and time) will I schedule that block of time:

_____

_____

_____

Make sure you add that block of time in your schedule as you would for an important appointment.

6. Focus on one big project at a time

Are you focusing on too many things at once? If you had to focus on only one major project at a time, what would that be and why?

What major project I would focus on:

_____

Why:

_____

_____

_____

_____

To identify the right projects, ask yourself the question below:

If I had to stick to only one project with no guarantee I could ever work on any other project on my list, which one would I pursue? And why?

_____

On a scale from 1 to 10, with 1 being not at all and 10 being extremely, how excited am I about each individual project?

0_____10

On a scale from 1 to 10, 1 being not at all and 10 being extremely, how confident I am in my ability to follow through and complete each project?

0_____10

When completed successfully, which project would make it easier to complete all your other projects?

_____

Which project will bring me the most joy?

_____

Which project aligns the closest with my values, personality and vision?

_____

7. Managing your energy the right way

One of the keys to becoming productive is to eat well, sleep well and exercise regularly.

Rate yourself on a scale of 1 to 10 (1 being awful, 10 being amazing)

Eating habits

0 _____ 10

Sleeping habits

0 _____ 10

Exercising habits

0 _____ 10

Now, if you could select only one area to improve on, what would that be? Nutrition, sleep or exercise?

_____

What one thing could you do in particular to improve that area?

_____

Taking break

Experiment with the techniques below. For instance, you can choose one technique and test it for a week :

1. Every 75 - 90 minutes with 15-minute breaks
2. Every 52 minutes with 10 to 15-minute breaks
3. Every 25 minutes with 5-minute breaks

Which technique will you try in the next seven days?

_____

PART V

DESTROYING THE SHINY OBJECT SYNDROME

Are you a victim of the Shiny Object Syndrome? On a scale of 1 to 10 how true the statements below are for you (1 being false 10 being true)

1. I tend to believe in the magic pill

0 _____ 10

2. I often get high when I start something new

0 _____ 10

3. I'd rather give up than finding out I'm not good as I thought

0 _____ 10

4. I often give up what I start looking for better solutions out there

0 _____ 10

5. I often spread myself too thin in an attempt to hedge my bet

0 _____ 10

Write down one goal you fail to achieve in the past 12 months:

_____

Did you fall for one of the five pitfalls above? If so, which one?

_____

Overcoming the Shiny Object Syndrome

Do you often jump from one thing to the next?

Come up with one example of your personal life to illustrate each of the four scenarios below:

1. Jumping from one goal to another:

_____
_____
_____
_____

2. Jumping from one course to another (with the same goal):

_____
_____
_____
_____

3. Jumping from one tactic to another:

_____

_____

_____

_____

4. Jumping from one type of material to another:

_____

_____

_____

_____

Assessing the value of information

To find the right information, ask yourself the following questions:

- Is there anyone I know who has achieved that goal/has the right information or knows someone who has?
- Who can I pay to achieve the results I want or find the information I need?
- What course can I buy to save time and maximize the chances I obtain the information I need?
- What are one or two of the best books ever written in the topic I want to learn about? And who might know what these books are?

How to select the right course

To ensure you invest in the right course or product, ask yourself the following questions:

- Is this product what I need to achieve my current goal
- Is this product for me? Do you have the skills, mindset, motivation, time and personality required to make the most of this product?
- Is now the right timing? You might need to do other things first.
- Am I willing to commit until I achieve results

How to evaluate the value of a product

Using the table below, write down products, courses or services you bought in the past twelve months. Then, when relevant, write down the time saved, money made, mentally energy spread and emotional benefit received.

Product/service	Hours saved	Extra money made	Mental energy spared	Emotional benefits received

Before buying any product evaluate its value using the following criteria:

- Time: How much time can it allow you to save?
- Money: How much money can it allow you to generate or save?
- Energy: How much mental energy can it spare you (confusion, effort spent on gathering the right information etc.)
- Well-being: What emotional benefits can it bring you (peace of mind, confidence etc.)

Developing a mastery mindset

Write down five things that you may know very well intellectually but haven't really mastered. To do so, look at areas in your life where you haven't been able to achieve the results you want.

Your five things:

1.
2.
3.
4.
5.

The 7 Pillars of the mastery mindset

Are you a master or a dabbler? For each statement below rate yourself on a scale of 1 to 10 (1 being false 10 being true)

1. I'm a master of repetition

0 _____ 10

2. I master the fundamentals

0 _____ 10

3. I trust the process and keep going until I achieve results

0 _____ 10

4. I am willing to learn

0 _____ 10

5. I always think long-term

0 _____ 10

6. I'm consistent in everything I do

0 _____ 10

7. I'm extremely focused

0 _____ 10

7 steps to scheduling your learning

Whatever you're trying to learn, for maximum effectiveness, make sure you schedule your learning using the following steps:

1. Decide exactly what you need to learn
2. Find the most suitable course, book or program
3. Set a specific target
4. Choose how much time you'll spend studying (and be consistent)
5. Schedule blocks of time for your learning each week
6. Practice active learning by implementing what you learn
7. Make it a daily habit. Whenever possible, practice what you learn every day to fully integrate it.

PART VI

OVERCOMING PROCRASTINATION ONCE AND FOR ALL

10 Steps to overcome procrastination

1. Understand what's hidden behind procrastination.
2. Identify your story.
3. Rewrite your story..
4. Identify all the ways you distract yourself.
5. Clarify your why.
6. Start small.
7. Create daily habits to support you.
8. Prepare your environment.
9. Set small milestones and celebrate small wins.
10. Just get started.

Choose one task you tend to procrastinate on. Then, go through the 10 steps below.

1.Understand what's hidden behind procrastination. Uncover whether you procrastinate because of fear, lack of clarity or motivation, insufficient accountability or poor discipline.

Why you procrastinate:

_____

_____

_____

_____

2. Identify your story. Find out all the excuses you tell yourself

Your excuses:

_____

_____

_____

_____

3. Rewrite your story. Put in place empowering affirmations instead of your current excuses.

Your affirmation(s):

_____

_____

_____

_____

4. Identify all the ways you distract yourself. Become aware of the stratagems you rely on to distract yourself and put off your tasks.

You distract yourself by:

_____

_____

_____

_____

5. Clarify your why. Change the meaning you give to your tasks so that you feel more inspired and motivated.

Your new empowering meaning:

_____

_____

_____

_____

6. Start small. Set tiny goals to avoid resistance.

Your tiny goal:

_____

7. Create daily habits to support you. Implement habits so that you work on your most important tasks first thing in the morning.

Your daily habits:

_____

_____

_____

8. Prepare your environment. Reduce frictions in your environment and make it as easy as possible to take the desired action.

You'll reduce friction by:

_____
_____
_____
_____

9. Set small milestones and celebrate small wins. Break down daunting tasks into smaller tasks that you can easily achieve. Then, celebrate your daily wins.

Your small tasks:

_____
_____
_____
_____

10. Just get started. Begin working on your tasks while giving yourself permission to give up at any time.

How to overcome perfectionism

To overcome perfectionism keep in the mind the following points:

1. You are exactly where you're supposed to be doing exactly what you're supposed to do
2. You can always get better
3. You're doing okay

Closing open loops

When you feel stuck, complete one of the two things below:

1. Write down all the things you need to do. Then schedule a block of time and complete as many as possible. You can use the blank pages at the end of this workbook to do so.
2. Identify the one task you've been putting off for too long and complete it.

17 strategies to boost your focus

A. Know what you want

Gaining clarity regarding what you want will allow you to set the right priorities, placing your focus where it needs to be.

1. Find your strengths. Take time to identify what you're good at and enjoy doing.

2. Uncover your passion. Discover what you're passionate about.

3. Identify your core values. Create a list of your top core values and strive to live by them every day.

4. Create a long-term vision for your life. Spend time to craft a compelling vision that you can break down into smaller tasks to complete each day and each week.

B. Plan effectively

Planning will help you move from one task to the next, while avoiding becoming overly distracted.

5. Plan your day. Start your day by writing down the few key tasks you want to complete that day.

6. Write down your goals. Write your goals in a notebook and leave it open on your desk so that you can see it. Read the list whenever you start feeling distracted.

7. Carve out uninterrupted blocks of time. Schedule blocks of time to focus on your most important project(s), and make sure you are not interrupted.

C. Build momentum

Generate momentum by putting in place effective daily routines.

8. Make the correct domino fall. Implement one daily habit that will make it easier for you to achieve your goals.

9. Implement a morning ritual. Put in place a daily ritual. Make sure it helps you maximize your focus. For instance, this could be by starting with your major tasks or doing meditation.

D. Reduce distractions

Minimize distractions by using the "power of less."

10. Focus only on a few key goals. Remove goals that aren't absolute priorities, so you can give your undivided attention to your major goals.

11. Complete a digital detox. Avoid checking your digital devices first thing in the morning. Instead, create a morning ritual that includes your most important tasks.

12. Batch distracting activities together. Create a daily routine that includes all your distracting activities such as visiting social media, answering emails or web surfing, to minimize your daily distractions.

13. Empty your inbox. Unsubscribe from all your newsletters except the few you're actually reading and enjoying. Do this regularly—at least monthly.

14. Optimize your environment. Get rid of everything that has the potential to distract you. Clean your desk, turn off your phone, close unnecessary windows on your computer, et cetera.

15. Say "No" more often. Learn to decline requests that aren't in line with your values and goals.

E. Manage your energy well

Make effective use of your energy to increase your focus and boost your productivity.

16. Master the fundamentals. Sleep well, eat well and exercise regularly. These are fundamental to boosting your energy and enhancing your focus.

17. Make the most of peak energy levels. Make sure you work on your key tasks when you have the most energy available. For many people, this is in the morning.

Implement these strategies and you'll see your focus improve over time. Remember, you can either be focused or distracted, but you can't be both at the same time.

Conclusion

That's the end of the workbook.

I hope you benefited from doing the exercises in it. Don't hesitate to revisit the book and workbook whenever necessary. Remember, one of the pillars of the Mastery Mindset is repetition.

If you have any questions, email me at:

thibaut.meurisse@gmail.com

I wish you all the best with your future endeavors.

Thibaut Meurisse

NOTES:

Master Your Life With The Mastery Series

This book is the third book in the **"Mastery Series"**. You can check the other books at the following URL:

mybook.to/mastery_series

MASTER YOUR EMOTIONS (PREVIEW)

> The mind in its own place, and in itself can make a heaven of Hell, a hell of Heaven.
>
> — JOHN MILTON, POET.

We all experience a wild range of emotions throughout our lives. I had to admit, while writing this book, I experienced highs and lows myself. At first, I was filled with excitement and thrilled at the idea of providing people with a guide to help them understand their emotions. I imagined how readers' lives would improve as they learned to control their emotions. My motivation was high and I couldn't help but imagine how great the book would be.

Or so I thought.

After the initial excitement, the time came to sit down to write the actual book, and that's when the excitement wore off pretty quickly. Ideas that looked great in my mind suddenly felt dull. My writing seemed boring, and I felt as though I had nothing substantive or valuable to contribute.

Sitting at my desk and writing became more challenging each day. I started losing confidence. Who was I to write a book about emotions if I couldn't even master my own emotions? How ironic! I considered giving up. There are already plenty of books on the topic, so why add one more?

At the same time, I realized this book was a perfect opportunity to work on my own emotional issues. And who doesn't suffer from negative emotions from time to time? We all have highs and lows, don't we? The key is what we *do* with our lows. Are we using our emotions to grow? Are we learning something from them? Or are we beating ourselves up over them?

So, let's talk about *your* emotions now. Let me start by asking you this:

How do you feel right now?

Knowing how you feel is the first step toward taking control of your emotions. You may have spent so much time internalizing you've lost touch with your emotions. Perhaps you answered as follows: "I feel this book could be useful," or "I really feel I could learn something from this book." However, none of these answers reflect how you feel. You don't 'feel like this,' or 'feel like that,' you simply 'feel.' You don't 'feel like' this book could be useful, you 'think' this book could be useful, and that generates an emotion which makes you 'feel' excited about reading it. Feelings manifest as physical sensations in your body, not as an idea in your mind. Perhaps, the reason the word 'feel' is so often overused or misused is because we don't want to talk about our emotions. So, how do you feel now?

Why is it important to talk about emotions?

How you feel determines the quality of your life. Your emotions can make your life miserable or truly magical. That's why they are among the most important things to focus on. Your emotions color all your experiences. When you feel good, everything seems, feels, or tastes better. You also think better thoughts. Your energy levels are higher and possibilities seem limitless. Conversely, when you feel depressed, everything seems dull. You have little energy and you become unmotivated. You feel stuck in a place (mentally and physically) you don't want to be, and the future looks gloomy.

Your emotions can also act as a powerful guide. They can tell you something is wrong and allow you to make changes in your life. As such, they may be among the most powerful personal growth tools you have.

Sadly, neither your teachers nor your parents taught you how emotions work or how to control them. I find it ironic that just about anything comes with a how-to manual, while your mind doesn't. You've never received an instruction manual to teach you how your mind works and how to use it to better manage your emotions, have you? I haven't. In fact, until now, I doubt one even existed.

What you'll learn in this book

This book is the how-to manual your parents should have given you at birth. It's the instruction manual you should have received at school. In it, I'll share everything you need to know about emotions so you can overcome your fears and limitations and become the type of person you really want to be.

You'll learn what emotions are, how they are formed, and how you can use them for your personal growth. You'll also learn how to deal with negative emotions and condition your mind to create more positive emotions.

It is my sincere hope and expectation that, by the end of this book, you will have a clear understanding of what emotions are and will have all the tools you need to start taking control of them.

More specifically, this book will help you:

- Understand what emotions are and how they impact your life
- Identify negative emotions that control your life and learn to overcome them
- Change your story to take better control over your life and create a more compelling future, and
- Reprogram your mind to experience more positive emotions.

Here is a more detailed summary of what you'll learn in this book:

In **Part I**, we'll discuss what emotions are. You'll learn why you are wired to focus on negativity and what you can do to counter this effect. You'll also discover how your beliefs impinge upon your emotions. Finally, you'll learn how negative emotions work and why they are so tricky.

In **Part II**, we'll go over the things that directly impact your emotions. You'll understand the roles your body, your thoughts, your words, or your sleep, play in your life and how you can use them to change your emotions.

In **Part III**, you'll learn how emotions are formed. You'll also learn how to condition your mind to experience more positive emotions.

And finally, in **Part IV**, we'll discuss how to use your emotions as a tool for personal growth. You'll learn why you experience emotions such as fear or depression and how they work. You'll then discover how to use them to grow.

I. What emotions are

Have you ever wondered what emotions are and what purpose they serve?

In this section, we'll discuss how your survival mechanism affects your emotions. Then, we'll explain what the 'ego' is and how it impacts your emotions. Finally, we'll discover the mechanism behind emotions and learn why negative emotions can be so hard to deal with.

1. How your survival mechanism affects your emotions

Why people have a bias towards negativity

Your brain is designed for survival, which explains why you're able to read this book at this very moment. When you think about it, the probability of you being born was extremely low. For this miracle to happen, all the generations before you had to survive long enough to procreate. In their quest for survival and procreation, they must have faced death hundreds or perhaps thousands of times.

Fortunately, unlike your ancestors, you're (probably) not facing death every day. In fact, in many parts of the world, life has never been safer. Yet, your survival mechanism hasn't changed much. Your brain still scans your environment looking for potential threats.

In many ways, some parts of your brain have become obsolete. While you may not be seconds away from being eaten by a predator, your brain still gives significantly more weight to negative events than to positive ones.

Fear of rejection is one example of a bias toward negativity. In the past, being rejected from your tribe would reduce your chances of survival significantly. Therefore, you learned to look for any sign of rejection, and this became hardwired in your brain.

Nowadays, being rejected often carries little or no consequence to your long-term survival. You could be hated by the entire world and still have a job, a roof and plenty of food on the table, yet, your brain is still programmed to perceive rejection as a threat to your survival.

This is why rejection can be so painful. While you know most rejections are no big deal, you nevertheless feel the emotional pain. If you listen to your mind, you may even create a whole drama around it. You may believe you aren't worthy of love and dwell on a rejection for days or weeks. Worse still, you may become depressed as a result of this rejection.

In fact, one single criticism can often outweigh hundreds of positive ones. That's why, an author with fifty 5-star reviews, is likely to feel terrible when they receive a single 1-star review. While the author understands the 1-star review isn't a threat to her survival, her authorial brain doesn't. It likely interprets the negative review as a threat to her ego which triggers an emotional reaction.

The fear of rejection can also lead you to over-dramatize events. If your boss criticized you at work, your brain may see the event as a threat and you now think, "What if I'm fired? What if I can't find a job quickly enough and my wife leaves me? What about my kids?

What if I can't see them again?" While you are fortunate to have such an effective survival mechanism, it is also your responsibility to separate real threats from imaginary ones. If you don't, you'll experience unnecessary pain and worry that will negatively impact the quality of your life. To overcome this bias towards negativity, you must reprogram your mind. One of a human being's greatest powers is our ability to use our thoughts to shape our reality and interpret events in a more empowering way. This book will teach you how to do this.

Why your brain's job isn't to make you happy

Your brain's primary job is not to make you happy, but to ensure your survival. Thus, if you want to be happy, you must take control of your emotions rather than hoping you'll be happy because it's your natural state. In the following section, we'll discuss what happiness is and how it works.

How dopamine can mess with your happiness

Dopamine is a neurotransmitter which, among other functions, plays a major role in rewarding certain behaviors. When dopamine is released into specific areas of your brain—the pleasure centers—you get a high. This is what happens during exercise, when you gamble, have sex, or eat great food.

One of the roles of dopamine is to ensure you look for food so you don't die of starvation, and you search for a mate so you can reproduce. Without dopamine, our species would likely be extinct by now. It's a pretty good thing, right?

Well, yes and no. In today's world, this reward system is, in many cases, obsolete. While in the past, dopamine was linked to our survival instinct, The release of dopamine can now be generated artificially. A great example of this effect is social media, which uses psychology to suck as much time as possible out of your life. Have you noticed all these notifications that pop up constantly? They're used to trigger a release of dopamine so you stay connected, and the longer you stay connected, the more money the services make. Watching pornography or gambling also leads to a release of dopamine which can make these activities highly addictive.

Fortunately, we don't need to act each time our brain releases dopamine. For instance, we don't need to constantly check our Facebook newsfeeds just because it gives us a pleasurable shot of dopamine.

Today's society is selling a version of happiness that can make us *un*happy. We've become addicted to dopamine largely because of marketers who have found effective ways to exploit our brains. We receive multiple shots of dopamine throughout the day and we love it. But is that the same thing as happiness?

Worse than that, dopamine can create real addictions with severe consequences on our health. Research conducted at Tulane University showed that, when given permission to self-stimulate their pleasure center, participants did it an average of forty times per minute. They chose the stimulation of their pleasure center over food, even refusing to eat when hungry!

Korean, Lee Seung Seop is an extreme case of this syndrome. In 2005, Mr Seop died after playing a video game for fifty-eight hours straight with very little food or water, and no sleep. The subsequent investigation concluded the cause of death was heart failure induced by exhaustion and dehydration. He was only twenty-eight years old.

To take control of your emotions, it is essential you understand the role dopamine plays and how it affects your happiness. Are you addicted to your phone? Are you glued to your TV? Or maybe you spend too much time playing video games. Most of us are addicted to something. For some people it's obvious, but for others, it's more subtle. For instance, you could be addicted to thinking. To better control your emotions, it is important to shed the light on your addictions as they can rob you of your happiness.

The 'one day I will' myth

Do you believe that one day you will achieve your dream and finally be happy? This is unlikely to happen. You may (and I hope you will) achieve your dream, but you won't live 'happily ever after.' This is just another trick your mind plays on you.

Your mind quickly acclimates to new situations, which is probably the result of evolution and our need to adapt continually in order to survive and reproduce. This is also probably why the new car or house you want will only make you happy for a while. Once the initial excitement wears off, you'll move on to crave the next exciting thing. This phenomenon is known as 'hedonic adaptation.'

How hedonic adaptation works

Let me share an interesting study that will likely change the way you see happiness. This study, which was conducted on lottery winners and paraplegics, was extremely eye-opening for me. Conducted in 1978, the investigation evaluated how winning the lottery or becoming a paraplegic influence happiness:

The study found that one year after the event, both groups were just as happy as they were beforehand. Yes, just as happy (or unhappy). You can find more about it by watching Dan Gilbert's Ted Talk, The Surprising Science of Happiness.

Perhaps you believe that you'll be happy once you've 'made it.' But, as the above study on happiness shows, this is simply not true. No matter what happens to you, you'll revert back to your predetermined level of happiness once you've adapted to the new event. This is how your mind works.

Does that mean you can't be happier than you are right now? No. What it means is that, in the long run, external events have very little impact upon your level of happiness.

In fact, according to Sonja Lyubomirsky, author of *The How of Happiness*, fifty percent of our happiness is determined by genetics, forty percent by internal factors, and only ten percent by external factors. These external factors include such things as whether we're single or married, rich or poor, and similar social influences.

This suggests, only ten percent of your happiness is linked to external factors, which is probably way less than you thought. The bottom line is this: Your attitude towards life influences your happiness, not what happens to you.

By now, you understand how your survival mechanism impacts negatively your emotions and prevent you from experiencing more joy and happiness in your life. In the next segment/section we'll learn about the ego.

To read more visit my author page at:

amazon.com/author/thibautmeurisse

Made in United States
Orlando, FL
09 March 2025